WELCOME to LONDON

FIRST PUBLISHED 2017 BY BUTTON BOOKS, AN IMPRINT
OF GUILD OF MASTER CRAFTSMAN PUBLICATIONS LTD,
CASTLE PLACE, 166 HIGH STREET, LEWES,
EAST SUSSEX BN7 1XU, UK

ILLUSTRATIONS © MARCOS FARINA, 2017
COPYRIGHT IN THE WORK © GMC PUBLICATIONS
LTD, 2017

ISBN 978 1 90898 581 1

DISTRIBUTED BY PUBLISHERS GROUP WEST IN THE
UNITED STATES.

A CATALOGUE RECORD FOR THIS BOOK IS AVAILABLE
FROM THE BRITISH LIBRARY.

PUBLISHER: JONATHAN BAILEY
PRODUCTION MANAGER: JIM BULLEY
SENIOR PROJECT EDITOR: WENDY McANGUS
MANAGING ART EDITOR: GILDA PACITTI

COLOUR ORIGINATION BY GMC REPROGRAPHICS
PRINTED AND BOUND IN TURKEY

WELCOME to LONDON

Illustrated by

MARCOS FARINA

Button
BOOKS

You can travel all over the UK by train from London and even to other countries through a tunnel that goes under the sea.

At the station people
are rushing and waiting.

London is full of people
bustling from here to there.

There are police officers, buskers, business people, chimney sweeps and queens (pearly and royal) in London. How many of these characters have you met?

The height of
Nelson's Column
is 52m (170ft).

From the top,
  Nelson can see lions,
    people and lots of pigeons.

People love to watch Changing
the Guard at Buckingham Palace.

This is where the Queen lives. You can tell she's at home
because the Royal Standard flag is flying.

The ravens who live at the Tower of London are very important,
as legend has it that the tower will fall if they leave.

The Queen keeps the Crown Jewels there, and the guards,
known as Beefeaters, look after them.

TOWER BRIDGE

The River Thames goes right through the city so Londoners use bridges to cross back and forth. There are 33 bridges in total.

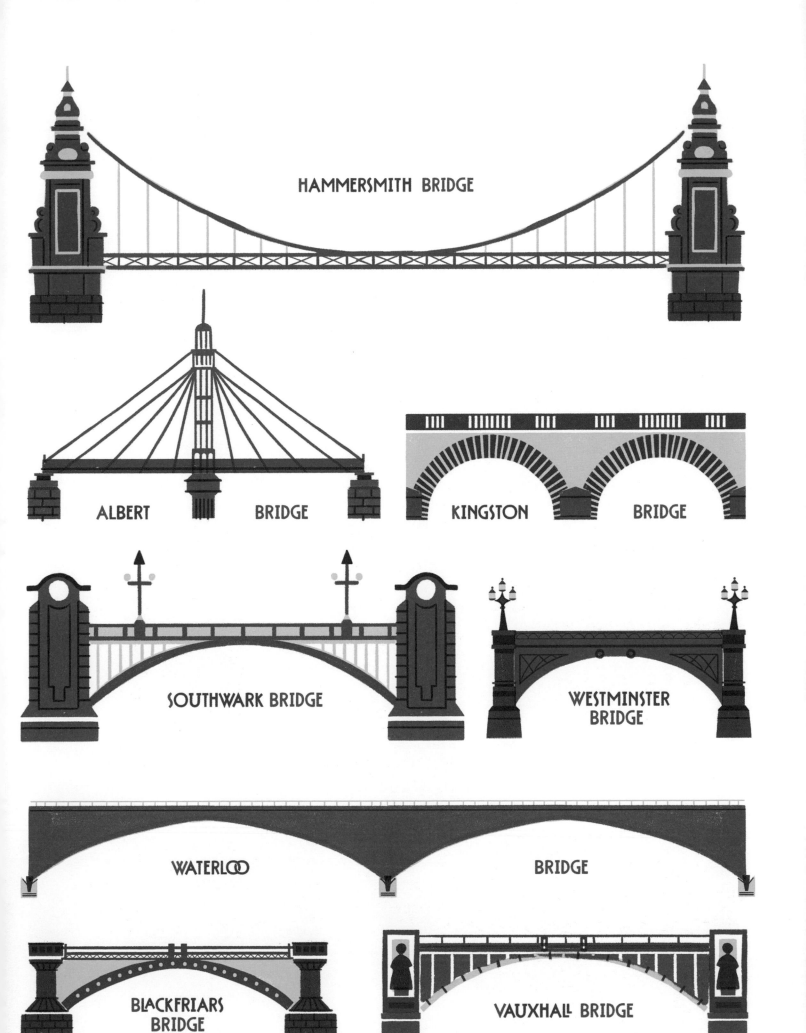

HAMMERSMITH BRIDGE

ALBERT BRIDGE

KINGSTON BRIDGE

SOUTHWARK BRIDGE

WESTMINSTER BRIDGE

WATERLOO BRIDGE

BLACKFRIARS BRIDGE

VAUXHALL BRIDGE

In Hyde Park lots of amazing trees grow. What sorts of trees have you seen today?

The Natural History Museum is teeming with wonders
from the world around us. But they won't bite.

The galleries in London
are packed with beautiful
and strange things to look at.

What's your favourite thing that you've seen?

There are **38** theatres
in London's West End.

At the theatre you can
travel to another world

full of music and
fun and excitement.

You can shop
till you drop,

or just
window shop

at the huge London
department stores.

At Covent Garden
there are

jugglers, cafés,
buskers and shops.

There's no garden now
but up until the 16th century
monks had a walled garden on this site.

The Prime Minister lives
at 10 Downing Street.

This is round the corner from
the Palace of Westminster

where important things
happen while Big Ben goes "Bong".

St Paul's Cathedral is one
of the monumental works

by 17th-century architect
Sir Christopher Wren.

At Westminster Abbey real-life fairy-tale weddings happen.
And almost every British monarch since 1066 has been crowned here.

COFFEE SHOP

ROYAL FESTIVAL HALL

**Relax by the river and watch the
crowds walking and skating past the Royal Festival Hall.**

Stroll along the South Bank
and play I Spy

on the London Eye.
What can you see?

Since it opened in 1871 the Royal Albert Hall has hosted all sorts of exciting events, including the Proms and concerts by The Beatles.

If you're hungry then Borough Market is the place to be!
There are stalls with every kind of food you can imagine.

POTATOES
APPLES
PUMPKINS
RADISHES

BOROUGH market

fish

There are all sorts of different tasty things to eat in London.

What food have you eaten?

What was your favourite thing?

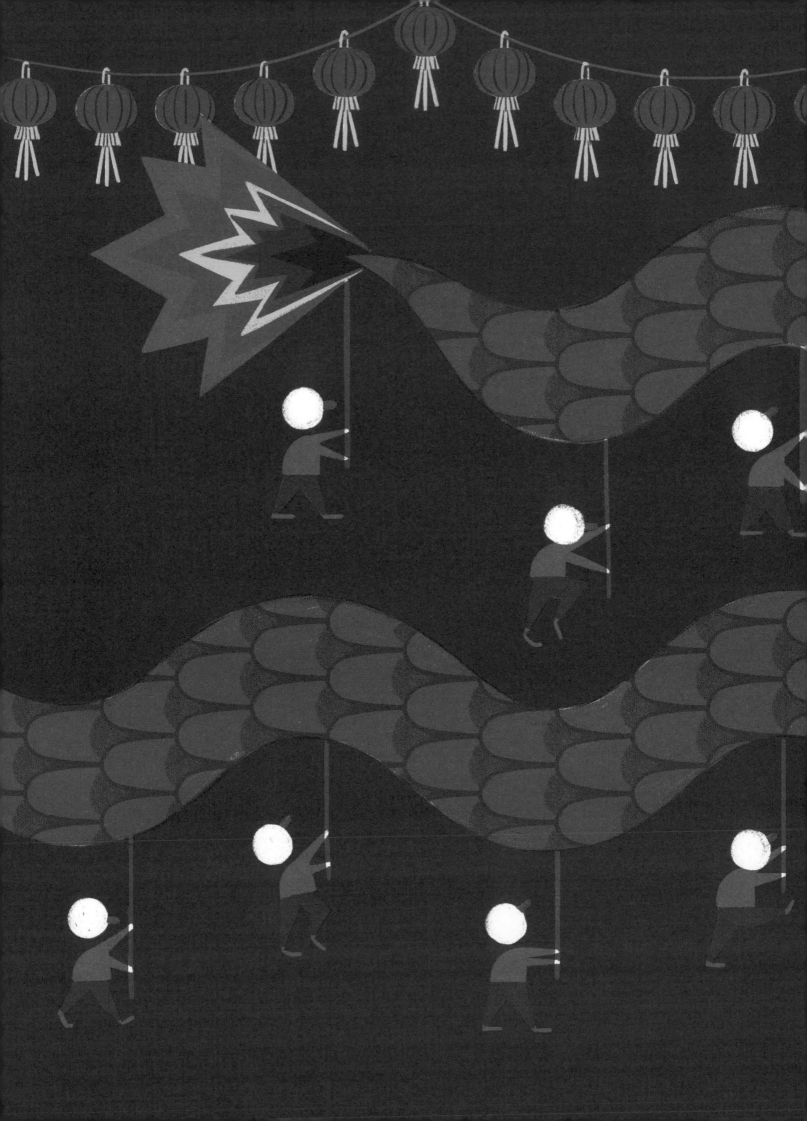

If you wander around Chinatown you might
think you are in Beijing not London!

Camden Town is packed with shops,
cafés and interesting people.

The markets held at Camden Lock are popular
with visitors from all over the world.

Greenwich is home to special clocks, telescopes and ships.

So take your time here and learn about adventures in science and on the sea.

CUTTY SARK

At Kew Gardens there are huge glass houses,
a treetop walkway and even a giant pagoda.

London is very sporty. Every year the city hosts Wimbledon, the oldest tennis tournament in the world, and there's Lord's, the home of cricket.

Wembley is the most famous English football ground.

ADDER

BUSHBABY

CATFISH

DUCK

EAGLE

FLAMINGO

GOAT

HIPPO

IGUANA

JELLYFISH

KOMODO DRAGON

LEMUR

MONKEY

NEWT

OWL

PENGUIN

QUEEN BEE

RABBIT

SPIDER

TIGER

UARU

VICUGNA

WARTHOG

XENOPUS LONGIPES FROG

YAMATO SHRIMP

ZEBRA

Henry VIII lived at Hampton Court Palace.
Here's how to remember what happened to his wives:

King Henry the Eighth to six wives he was wedded.
One died, one survived, two divorced, two beheaded.

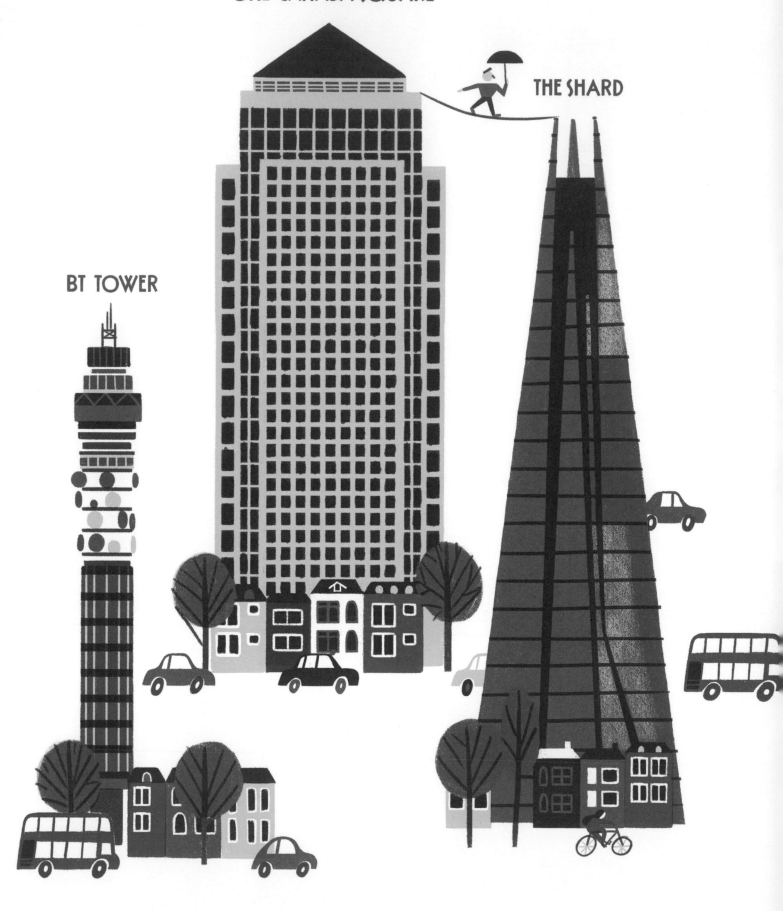

ONE CANADA SQUARE

THE SHARD

BT TOWER

If you look up when you're walking around London,
some of the buildings are so high you can't see the top of them.

110 BISHOPSGATE

30 ST MARY AXE
(THE GHERKIN)

122 LEADENHALL STREET
(THE CHEESEGRATER)

For more on Button Books, contact:

GMC PUBLICATIONS LTD
CASTLE PLACE, 166 HIGH STREET, LEWES, EAST SUSSEX, BN7 1XU
UNITED KINGDOM
TEL +44 (0)1273 488005
WWW.BUTTONBOOKS.CO.UK